Great Works Instructional Guides for Literature

Charlotte's Web

A guide for the book by E. B. White
Great Works Author: Debra J. Housel, M.S.Ed.

SHELL EDUCATION

Publishing Credits

Corinne Burton, M.A.Ed., *President*; Emily R. Smith, M.A.Ed., *Editorial Director*; Lee Aucoin, *Multimedia Designer*;
Jill K. Mulhall, M.Ed., *Editor*; Stephanie Bernard, *Assistant Editor*; Don Tran, *Production Artist*; Amber Goff, *Editorial Assistant*

Image Credits

Shutterstock (cover, pages 20, 39); Timothy J. Bradley (pages 28, 46, 55, 61–64)

Standards

© 2007 Teachers of English to Speakers of Other Languages, Inc. (TESOL)
© 2007 Board of Regents of the University of Wisconsin System. World-Class Instructional Design and Assessment (WIDA)
© Copyright 2010. National Governors Association Center for Best Practices and Council of Chief State School Officers.
All rights reserved.

Shell Education

5301 Oceanus Drive
Huntington Beach, CA 92649-1030
http://www.shelleducation.com
ISBN 978-1-4807-6995-3
© 2015 Shell Educational Publishing, Inc.

Table of Contents

How to Use This Literature Guide

Today's standards demand rigor and relevance in the reading of complex texts. The units in this series guide teachers in a rich and deep exploration of worthwhile works of literature for classroom study. The most rigorous instruction can also be interesting and engaging!

Many current strategies for effective literacy instruction have been incorporated into these instructional guides for literature. Throughout the units, text-dependent questions are used to determine comprehension of the book as well as student interpretation of the vocabulary words. The books chosen for the series are complex and are exemplars of carefully crafted works of literature. Close reading is used throughout the units to guide students toward revisiting the text and using textual evidence to respond to prompts orally and in writing. Students must analyze the story elements in multiple assignments for each section of the book. All of these strategies work together to rigorously guide students through their study of literature.

The next few pages describe how to use this guide for a purposeful and meaningful literature study. Each section of this guide is set up in the same way to make it easier for you to implement the instruction in your classroom.

Theme Thoughts

The great works of literature used throughout this series have important themes that have been relevant to people for many years. Many of the themes will be discussed during the various sections of this instructional guide. However, it would also benefit students to have independent time to think about the key themes of the book.

Before students begin reading, have them complete the *Pre-Reading Theme Thoughts* (page 13). This graphic organizer will allow students to think about the themes outside the context of the story. They'll have the opportunity to evaluate statements based on important themes and defend their opinions. Be sure to keep students' papers for comparison to the *Post-Reading Theme Thoughts* (page 59). This graphic organizer is similar to the pre-reading activity. However, this time, students will be answering the questions from the point of view of one of the characters in the book. They have to think about how the character would feel about each statement and defend their thoughts. To conclude the activity, have students compare what they thought about the themes before they read the book to what the characters discovered during the story.

Litter-at-ure

How to Use This Literature Guide (cont.)

Vocabulary

Each teacher reference vocabulary overview page has definitions and sentences about how key vocabulary words are used in the section. These words should be introduced and discussed with students. Students will use these words in different activities throughout the book.

On some of the vocabulary student pages, students are asked to answer text-related questions about vocabulary words from the sections. The following question stems will help you create your own vocabulary questions if you'd like to extend the discussion.

- How does this word describe _____'s character?
- How does this word connect to the problem in this story?
- How does this word help you understand the setting?
- Tell me how this word connects to the main idea of this story.
- What visual pictures does this word bring to your mind?
- Why do you think the author used this word?

At times, you may find that more work with the words will help students understand their meanings and importance. These quick vocabulary activities are a good way to further study the words.

- Students can play vocabulary concentration. Make one set of cards that has the words on them and another set with the definitions. Then, have students lay them out on the table and play concentration. The goal of the game is to match vocabulary words with their definitions. For early readers or English language learners, the two sets of cards could be the words and pictures of the words.

- Students can create word journal entries about the words. Students choose words they think are important and then describe why they think each word is important within the book. Early readers or English language learners could instead draw pictures about the words in a journal.

- Students can create puppets and use them to act out the vocabulary words from the stories. Students may also enjoy telling their own character-driven stories using vocabulary words from the original stories.

How to Use This Literature Guide (cont.)

Analyzing the Literature

After you have read each section with students, hold a small-group or whole-class discussion. Provided on the teacher reference page for each section are leveled questions. The questions are written at two levels of complexity to allow you to decide which questions best meet the needs of your students. The Level 1 questions are typically less abstract than the Level 2 questions. These questions are focused on the various story elements, such as character, setting, and plot. Be sure to add further questions as your students discuss what they've read. For each question, a few key points are provided for your reference as you discuss the book with students.

Reader Response

In today's classrooms, there are often great readers who are below average writers. So much time and energy is spent in classrooms getting students to read on grade level that little time is left to focus on writing skills. To help teachers include more writing in their daily literacy instruction, each section of this guide has a literature-based reader response prompt. Each of the three genres of writing is used in the reader responses within this guide: narrative, informative/explanatory, and opinion. Before students write, you may want to allow them time to draw pictures related to the topic.

Guided Close Reading

Within each section of this guide, it is suggested that you closely reread a portion of the text with your students. Page numbers are given, but since some versions of the books may have different page numbers, the sections to be reread are described by location as well. After rereading the section, there are a few text-dependent questions to be answered by students.

Working space has been provided to help students prepare for the group discussion. They should record their thoughts and ideas on the activity page and refer to it during your discussion. Rather than just taking notes, you may want to require students to write complete responses to the questions before discussing them with you.

Encourage students to read one question at a time and then go back to the text and discover the answer. Work with students to ensure that they use the text to determine their answers rather than making unsupported inferences. Suggested answers are provided in the answer key.

How to Use This Literature Guide (cont.)

Guided Close Reading (cont.)

The generic open-ended stems below can be used to write your own text-dependent questions if you would like to give students more practice.

- What words in the story support . . . ?
- What text helps you understand . . . ?
- Use the book to tell why _____ happens.
- Based on the events in the story, . . . ?
- Show me the part in the text that supports . . . .
- Use the text to tell why . . . .

Making Connections

The activities in this section help students make cross-curricular connections to mathematics, science, social studies, fine arts, or other curricular areas. These activities require higher-order thinking skills from students but also allow for creative thinking.

Language Learning

A special section has been set aside to connect the literature to language conventions. Through these activities, students will have opportunities to practice the conventions of standard English grammar, usage, capitalization, and punctuation.

Story Elements

It is important to spend time discussing what the common story elements are in literature. Understanding the characters, setting, plot, and theme can increase students' comprehension and appreciation of the story. If teachers begin discussing these elements in early childhood, students will more likely internalize the concepts and look for the elements in their independent reading. Another very important reason for focusing on the story elements is that students will be better writers if they think about how the stories they read are constructed.

In the story elements activities, students are asked to create work related to the characters, setting, or plot. Consider having students complete only one of these activities. If you give students a choice on this assignment, each student can decide to complete the activity that most appeals to him or her. Different intelligences are used so that the activities are diverse and interesting to all students.

How to Use This Literature Guide (cont.)

Culminating Activity

At the end of this instructional guide is a creative culminating activity that allows students the opportunity to share what they've learned from reading the book. This activity is open ended so that students can push themselves to create their own great works within your language arts classroom.

Comprehension Assessment

The questions in this section require students to think about the book they've read as well as the words that were used in the book. Some questions are tied to quotations from the book to engage students and require them to think about the text as they answer the questions.

Response to Literature

Finally, students are asked to respond to the literature by drawing pictures and writing about the characters and stories. A suggested rubric is provided for teacher reference.

Correlation to the Standards

Shell Education is committed to producing educational materials that are research and standards based. As part of this effort, we have correlated all of our products to the academic standards of all 50 states, the District of Columbia, the Department of Defense Dependents Schools, and all Canadian provinces.

Purpose and Intent of Standards

Standards are designed to focus instruction and guide adoption of curricula. Standards are statements that describe the criteria necessary for students to meet specific academic goals. They define the knowledge, skills, and content students should acquire at each level. Standards are also used to develop standardized tests to evaluate students' academic progress. Teachers are required to demonstrate how their lessons meet standards. Standards are used in the development of all of our products, so educators can be assured they meet high academic standards.

How to Find Standards Correlations

To print a customized correlation report of this product for your state, visit our website at http://www.shelleducation.com and follow the online directions. If you require assistance in printing correlation reports, please contact our Customer Service Department at 1-877-777-3450.

Correlation to the Standards (cont.)

Standards Correlation Chart

The lessons in this book were written to support today's college and career readiness standards. The following chart indicates which lessons address each standard.

College and Career Readiness Standard	Section
Read closely to determine what the text says explicitly and to make logical inferences from it; cite specific textual evidence when writing or speaking to support conclusions drawn from the text. (R.1)	Guided Close Reading Sections 1–5
Determine central ideas or themes of a text and analyze their development; summarize the key supporting details and ideas. (R.2)	Analyzing the Literature Sections 1–5; Story Elements Sections 1–5; Post-Reading Theme Thoughts
Analyze how and why individuals, events, or ideas develop and interact over the course of a text. (R.3)	Analyzing the Literature Sections 1–5; Story Elements Sections 1–5
Interpret words and phrases as they are used in a text, including determining technical, connotative, and figurative meanings, and analyze how specific word choices shape meaning or tone. (R.4)	Vocabulary Sections 1–5
Analyze the structure of texts, including how specific sentences, paragraphs, and larger portions of the text (e.g., a section, chapter, scene, or stanza) relate to each other and the whole. (R.5)	Guided Close Reading Sections 1–5; Comprehension Assessment
Integrate and evaluate content presented in diverse media and formats, including visually and quantitatively, as well as in words. (R.7)	Making Connections Section 4
Read and comprehend complex literary and informational texts independently and proficiently. (R.10)	Entire Unit
Write arguments to support claims in an analysis of substantive topics or texts using valid reasoning and relevant and sufficient evidence. (W.1)	Reader Response Sections 3–4
Write informative/explanatory texts to examine and convey complex ideas and information clearly and accurately through the effective selection, organization, and analysis of content. (W.2)	Reader Response Sections 2, 5

College and Career Readiness Standard	Section
Write narratives to develop real or imagined experiences or events using effective technique, well-chosen details and well-structured event sequences. (W.3)	Reader Response Section 1; Culminating Activity
Produce clear and coherent writing in which the development, organization, and style are appropriate to task, purpose, and audience. (W.4)	Reader Response Sections 1–5; Response to Literature; Culminating Activity
Use technology, including the Internet, to produce and publish writing and to interact and collaborate with others. (W.6)	Culminating Activity
Demonstrate command of the conventions of standard English grammar and usage when writing or speaking. (L.1)	Language Learning Sections 1–5; Reader Response Sections 1–5
Demonstrate command of the conventions of standard English capitalization, punctuation, and spelling when writing. (L.2)	Language Learning Sections 1–5; Vocabulary Activity Section 1; Reader Response Sections 1–5
Determine or clarify the meaning of unknown and multiple-meaning words and phrases by using context clues, analyzing meaningful word parts, and consulting general and specialized reference materials, as appropriate. (L.4)	Vocabulary Sections 1–5
Demonstrate understanding of figurative language, word relationships, and nuances in word meanings. (L.5)	Vocabulary Sections 4–5
Acquire and use accurately a range of general academic and domain-specific words and phrases sufficient for reading, writing, speaking, and listening at the college and career readiness level; demonstrate independence in gathering vocabulary knowledge when encountering an unknown term important to comprehension or expression. (L.6)	Vocabulary Sections 1–5

TESOL and WIDA Standards

The lessons in this book promote English language development for English language learners. The following TESOL and WIDA English Language Development Standards are addressed through the activities in this book:

- **Standard 1:** English language learners communicate for social and instructional purposes within the school setting.

- **Standard 2:** English language learners communicate information, ideas and concepts necessary for academic success in the content area of language arts.

About the Author—E. B. White

Elwyn Brooks White was born in upstate New York in July 1899, the youngest of six children. He was never a fan of the name Elwyn; while a student at Cornell University he adopted the nickname "Andy," which is how he was known for the rest of his life. While at Cornell, White served as editor of *The Cornell Daily Sun*. After graduating in 1921, he embarked upon a career in journalism. After several years he landed a job with the prestigious *The New Yorker* magazine, where he stayed for the rest of his career.

White wrote a column for *The New Yorker* for more than half a century. He married Katharine Angell, a writer and editor at the magazine, in 1929. Over the years, White also authored and co-authored many books. He published his first children's book, *Stuart Little*, in 1945.

White spent much of his time at his family's secluded farm home in North Brooklin, Maine. One day he noticed a spider spinning an egg sac in the barn. This moment served as an inspiration for *Charlotte's Web*, which was first published in 1952. The book was received warmly and was named a Newbery Honor book. Over time, its popularity became massive. The book has been translated into 23 languages and inspired two movie adaptations (in 1973 and 2006).

In 1959, White edited and updated *The Elements of Style*, one of the most famous guides on English language grammar and style. In 2011, TIME listed *The Elements of Style* as one of the 100 best and most influential books written in English since 1923.

Despite the popularity of his books, White was fiercely private. He disliked publicity and avoided strangers, especially members of the press. While at the offices of *The New Yorker*, he would sometimes leave his office by going down the fire escape rather than talk to someone he didn't know.

In 1963, White was awarded the Presidential Medal of Freedom. In 1970, he was awarded the coveted Laura Ingalls Wilder Medal. This award is given to "an author or illustrator whose books, published in the United States, have, over a period of years, made a substantial and lasting contribution to literature for children." That same year he published his third children's classic, *The Trumpet of the Swan*. In 1971, White won the National Medal for Literature. He was elected to the American Academy of Arts and Letters in 1973. In 1978, he won a special Pulitzer Prize for his body of work.

White, who suffered from Alzheimer's disease, died in 1985 at the age of 86. His influence on children lives on, however. *Charlotte's Web* consistently appears as number one on lists of the top books for children.

Possible Texts for Text Comparisons

In addition to *Charlotte's Web*, E. B. White also wrote the classic children's novels *Stuart Little* and *The Trumpet of the Swan*. Either of these titles can be used in compelling studies of books by the same author.

Book Summary of *Charlotte's Web*

Eight-year-old Fern Arable is distressed when she realizes her father is about to kill the runt of a newly born pig litter. She convinces her father to spare the pig's life, on the condition that she will care for the piglet herself. Fern spends the next several weeks doting on the tiny pig, whom she calls Wilbur.

In time, Wilbur is sold to the owner of a neighboring farm and moves down the road. Wilbur is intrigued by his new home in a bustling barn full of animals, but he becomes lonely. He misses Fern and longs for a new friend. Wilbur soon finds that friend in Charlotte, a barn spider. At first, the pig worries that he can't be friends with a spider. But he soon realizes that Charlotte is clever, loving, and loyal.

During the summer, one of the sheep in the barn warns Wilbur that he will be killed for ham and bacon come wintertime. Wilbur is terrified until Charlotte promises that she will find a way to save his life. Charlotte eventually comes up with a plan to weave webs that spell out words that describe Wilbur. Her first web reads, "Some Pig." The special webs do the trick—people come from miles around to see them. They believe the web writing is a miracle and that Wilbur is a very unusual, special pig.

At the county fair in September, Wilbur wins a special prize that guarantees he can live his life free from worry of the ax. However, Charlotte, who accompanies him to the fair, dies. Heartbroken, Wilbur brings her egg sac home and watches over it lovingly all winter. When the baby spiders hatch, he is delighted, but when they form balloons and leave, he is overwhelmed by grief again. Three of Charlotte's daughters promise to stay with him and be his friends. Thus, Wilbur's life continues in a bittersweet cycle as each year a new set of Charlotte's progeny hatches and a few of the spiders stay with him, but none of them ever truly take Charlotte's place in his heart.

Cross-Curricular Connection

This book can be used in a unit about family, friendship, or domesticated animals; a unit about spiders and their life cycles; or when teaching about farm life in the mid-1900s.

Possible Texts for Text Sets

- Atwater, Richard and Florence. *Mr. Popper's Penguins*. Little, Brown Books for Young Readers, 1992.

- Cleary, Beverly. *Socks*. HarperCollins, 2008.

- Grahame, Kenneth. *The Wind in the Willows*. Dover Children's Evergreen Classics, 1999.

- King-Smith, Dick. *Babe: The Gallant Pig*. Random House Children's Books, 1995.

- Rawls, Wilson. *Summer of the Monkeys*. Yearling, 2010.

- Steig, William. *Abel's Island*. Square Fish, 2007.

Pre-Reading Theme Thoughts

Directions: Read each statement below. Draw a picture of a happy face or a sad face in the column next to it. The face should show how you feel about the statement. Then, use words to say what you think about each statement.

Statement	How Do You Feel? 😊 ☹️	Explain Your Answer
Spending time with animals can be enjoyable.	*(happy face drawn)*	It is nice
A loyal friend can be hard to find.	*(sad face drawn)*	Because a loyal friend could be right around the corner
Sometimes we have to say good-bye to a friend.	*(sad face drawn)*	Because I don't like loosing a friend
There is great joy simply in being alive.	*(happy face drawn)*	Because life if a gift from God.

Vocabulary Overview

Key words and phrases from this section are provided below with definitions and sentences about how the words are used in the story. Introduce and discuss these important vocabulary words with students. If you think these words or other words in the story warrant more time devoted to them, there are suggestions in the introduction for other vocabulary activities (page 5).

Word	Definition	Sentence about Text
sopping (ch. 1)	wet all the way through	Fern's sneakers are **sopping** after she walks through the wet grass.
injustice (ch. 1)	unfairness; wrong treatment	Fern insists it is an **injustice** to kill the piglet just because he is small.
specimen (ch. 1)	a notable example of something	Avery thinks that the runt is a miserable **specimen** of a pig.
manure (ch. 2)	farm animals' solid waste	Wilbur sleeps in a pile of **manure** in Zuckerman's barn.
perspiration (ch. 3)	sweat	The barn smells of hay, manure, and horse **perspiration**.
rooting (ch. 3)	digging in the earth with one's snout	Wilbur stops under an apple tree and begins digging and **rooting** for food.
appetizing (ch. 3)	appealing to one's sense of smell and taste	Mr. Zuckerman knows the smell of the slops will be **appetizing** to Wilbur.
fold (ch. 4)	a pen or a shelter for sheep	The sheep spend time in their **fold** when the weather is bad.
middlings (ch. 4)	a grain milling byproduct used in animal feed	Wheat **middlings** are usually a part of Wilbur's daily slops.
gnawing (ch. 4)	chewing	Templeton likes **gnawing** on things and making holes in them.
glutton (ch. 4)	one who frequently overeats	Templeton the rat admits that he is a **glutton** and will eat whatever he can find.
dejected (ch. 4)	feeling down; depressed	Wilbur stops eating because he feels lonely, friendless, and **dejected**.

Vocabulary Activity

Directions: Write five sentences about the story. Use one vocabulary word from the box below in each sentence.

Words from the Story

sopping	injustice	manure	perspiration	rooting
appetizing	fold	gnawing	glutton	dejected

_____

_____

_____

_____

_____

_____

_____

Directions: Answer this question.

1. Why does Avery think that Wilbur is a miserable **specimen** of a pig?

_____

_____

Analyzing the Literature

Provided below are discussion questions you can use in small groups, with the whole class, or for written assignments. Each question is written at two levels so that you can choose the right question for each group of students. For each question, a few key points are provided for your reference as you discuss the book with students.

Story Element	Level 1	Level 2	Key Discussion Points
Character	What emotions does Fern's father feel when Fern grabs hold of his ax?	How does Mr. Arable respond when Fern calls killing the pig an "injustice"?	At first Mr. Arable dismisses Fern's concerns. He is determined to kill the runt pig, claiming it will "make trouble." But when he sees how determined Fern is to save its life, and how strongly she feels, he is moved. He sees the situation through her eyes and almost cries himself. He decides to spare the pig.
Character	What does Avery say that shows his opinion of Fern's pig?	How is Avery's reaction to the runt pig different from Fern's reaction?	Avery calls the pig a "miserable thing" and sarcastically says that it's a fine specimen of a pig. He compares it to a white rat. While Fern is moved to protect and care for the pig, Avery doesn't have the same compassionate reaction. He just sees the pig as a funny, strange little thing.
Plot	Why does Mr. Arable tell Fern that she has to sell Wilbur?	What solution does Fern's mother suggest to help her feel better about losing Wilbur?	Fern raises Wilbur for five weeks. By that age, Wilbur has gotten bigger and needs more food. Mr. Arable is not willing to pay to feed him anymore. Fern cries about losing Wilbur. Mrs. Arable suggests that Fern sell the pig to her uncle, whose farm is just down the road. Fern can go visit Wilbur whenever she wants.
Setting	Where does Wilbur move at the beginning of chapter 3?	Where is Wilbur's new home located in Zuckerman's barn? Is it a nice spot?	Wilbur moves down the road to Mr. Zuckerman's farm. Zuckerman has a large, pleasant barn. Wilbur's pen is a manure pile in the lower part of the barn, underneath the cows. His new home is warm and comfortable.

Reader Response

Think

On a rainy day, Wilbur gets so lonely that he lies down and sobs. Think of a time when you felt lonely.

Narrative Writing Prompt

Write a note to yourself telling what you can do to cheer yourself up when you feel lonely.

_____

_____

_____

_____

_____

_____

_____

_____

_____

_____

Guided Close Reading

Closely reread the section in chapter 3 that begins with, "Now the trouble starts . . . ." Stop with, "He began to cry. "

Directions: Think about these questions. In the space below, write ideas or draw pictures as you think. Be ready to share your answers.

❶ What sentences in the text show that the other farm animals are delighted that Wilbur is out of his pen?

❷ Use details from the book to explain how Wilbur feels about being loose.

❸ How do you know that the people on the farm want Wilbur to return to his pen?

Making Connections-Meal Time!

- **Carnivores** are animals that eat other animals. They have sharp teeth to help them bite through meat.

- **Omnivores** are animals that eat both plants and meat. Omnivores have both sharp and flat teeth.

- **Herbivores** are animals that eat just plants. These animals have flat teeth to help grind down the plants.

Directions: Write three specific things that each farm animal would eat. If the animal can eat both meat and plants, write at least one of each.

Barn Cat—carnivore

-
-
-

Templeton—omnivore

-
-
-

Sheep—herbivore

-
-
-

Name _____ Date _____

Language Learning–Nouns and Proper Nouns

Directions: Decide which nouns below are proper nouns. Write each noun on the correct trough below. Be sure to capitalize the proper nouns.

Language Hints!

- Nouns name people, places, and things.
- Proper nouns are capitalized because they name specific people, places, and things.

lurvy	farmer	wilbur	sheep	templeton	avery
barn	pigpen	mrs. arable	rat	mr. zuckerman	goose

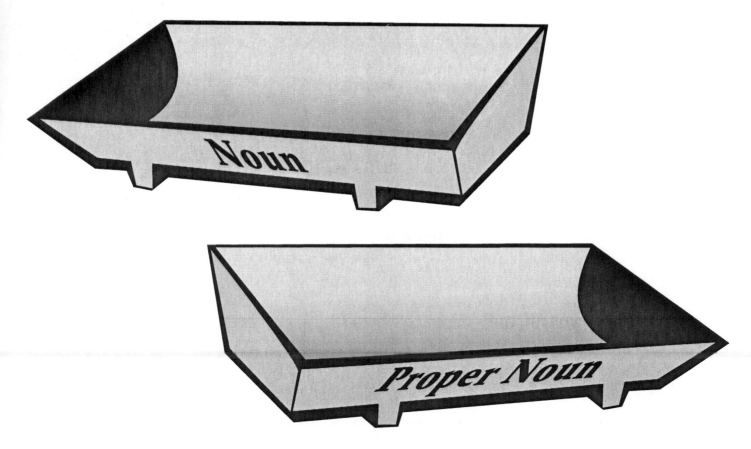

Story Elements-Plot

Directions: Based on the events in the story, fill in the columns of this graphic organizer.

Somebody wants	But	So
Mr. Arable wants to kill the runt pig.		
	Mr. Arable sells Wilbur to Mr. Zuckerman.	
		A voice promises to be Wilbur's friend.

Name _____ Date _____

Story Elements-Setting

Directions: Draw a map showing the Arable and Zuckerman farms and the path that Fern takes to walk from one to the other.

Vocabulary Overview

Key words and phrases from this section are provided below with definitions and sentences about how the words are used in the story. Introduce and discuss these important vocabulary words with students. If you think these words or other words in the story warrant more time devoted to them, there are suggestions in the introduction for other vocabulary activities (page 5).

Word	Definition	Sentence about Text
blundered (ch. 5)	moved clumsily or carelessly	Charlotte's sticky web traps the flies that **blunder** into it.
inheritance (ch. 5)	a trait that is derived genetically from one's ancestors	Charlotte's talent as a trapper is an **inheritance** from thousands of years of spiders.
scheming (ch. 5)	making secret plans, often devious ones	Wilbur worries he can't be friends with Charlotte because, as a spider, she is **scheming** and brutal.
swathes (ch. 6)	rows of grain or grass that fall when they get cut	**Swathes** of grass fall behind Mr. Zuckerman's mowing machine.
interlude (ch. 6)	a period of time between events	Summer is the **interlude** between spring and fall.
unremitting (ch. 6)	never stopping; incessant	After weeks of **unremitting** effort by the goose, her eggs finally hatch.
scruples (ch. 6)	uneasy feelings that make one hesitate to do things that are wrong	No one likes Templeton the rat because he has no **scruples**.
compunctions (ch. 6)	guilty feelings	Templeton does whatever he wants without any **compunctions**.
anaesthetic (ch. 7)	a substance that keeps one from feeling pain in one's body	Wilbur thinks it is thoughtful of Charlotte to inject her prey with an **anaesthetic** before she eats them.
conspiracy (ch. 7)	a plot; a secret plan made by two or more people in order to do something harmful	The old sheep warns Wilbur of a **conspiracy** by the people at the farm to kill him for food.
hysterics (ch. 7)	a wildly emotional, out-of-control reaction	Charlotte orders Wilbur to stop crying because she can't stand **hysterics**.
oblige (ch. 9)	to do a favor for someone in order to please him or her	Templeton gives Wilbur a piece of string, saying he is happy to **oblige**.

Name _____ Date _____

Vocabulary Activity

Directions: Draw lines to complete the sentences.

Sentence Beginnings	Sentence Endings
The spider injects an **anaesthetic**	ability to build a web and trap flies.
When the sheep says that Wilbur will die,	into each bug that **blunders** into her web.
Templeton seems happy to **oblige**	when Wilbur asks him for a piece of string.
The mowing machine leaves	**swathes** of hay in the field.
Charlotte's **inheritance** is the	the pig responds with **hysterics.**

Directions: Answer this question.

1. Who in the barn lacks **scruples**, and how do you know?

_____

_____

Analyzing the Literature

Provided below are discussion questions you can use in small groups, with the whole class, or for written assignments. Each question is written at two levels so that you can choose the right question for each group of students. For each question, a few key points are provided for your reference as you discuss the book with students.

Story Element	Level 1	Level 2	Key Discussion Points
Character	What does Wilbur think of Charlotte when he realizes she's a spider?	Why is Wilbur unsure at first about becoming friends with Charlotte?	Wilbur doesn't like the fact that Charlotte is a carnivore. He thinks that spinning a web and eating flies is cruel. He is not sure he wants to be friends with a spider because he considers them fierce, brutal, scheming, and bloodthirsty. Even though he is terribly lonely, he is not sure he can learn to like Charlotte.
Character	What do the animals in the barn think about Templeton the rat?	Why does the gander threaten Templeton?	The animals know that Templeton is a rat that has no scruples, no decency, and no kindness. He only cares about himself. The gander knows that Templeton would love to eat one of the goslings. He threatens the rat because he is worried that Templeton will kill one of the babies if he has the chance.
Plot	What does the old sheep tell Wilbur about Christmastime?	How does Wilbur react when the old sheep tells him what the future holds for him?	The old sheep tells Wilbur that he is being fattened up because he will be killed for meat at Christmastime. Wilbur becomes hysterical because he does not want to die. He cries and screams for someone to save him and races around his pigpen. He is very afraid.
Setting	What season is described at the beginning of chapter 6?	How are the early days of summer on a farm "the happiest and fairest days of the year"?	Chapter 6 includes a beautiful description of early summer on a farm. Lilacs and apple blossoms bloom and make the air smell sweet. The days grow warm and soft. The children have time to play and to help on the farm. Birds appear everywhere and fill the air with song. "Everywhere you look is life."

Name _____ Date _____

Reader Response

Think

Wilbur is afraid after the old sheep tells him he will be killed. Think about a time when you were scared.

Informative/Explanatory Writing Prompt

Describe a time when you were scared. What steps did you take to feel better? Did someone help you?

_____

_____

_____

_____

_____

_____

_____

_____

_____

_____

_____

Guided Close Reading

Closely reread the part at the end of chapter 5 where Charlotte talks about how she eats. Begin with, "Why not? It's true. . . ." Stop with, "Perhaps your web is a good thing after all."

Directions: Think about these questions. In the space below, write ideas or draw pictures as you think. Be ready to share your answers.

❶ According to Charlotte, why is she a trapper?

❷ Use details from the book to tell how Wilbur feels about Charlotte's eating habits.

❸ How does Charlotte explain why her feeding habits are necessary for the good of all animals?

Name _____   Date _____

Making Connections–The Parts of an Egg

In the story, seven goslings hatch from their mother's eggs. Inside an egg, an embryo grows into a gosling. It absorbs nutrients from the yolk and the egg white. Although it is hard, the shell lets air move in and out of the egg. As the gosling grows, it breathes.

Directions: Use books or the Internet to find a diagram of an egg. Then, label the parts of an egg in the spaces below.

Word Bank

yolk	air cell	inner membrane
shell	egg white	outer membrane

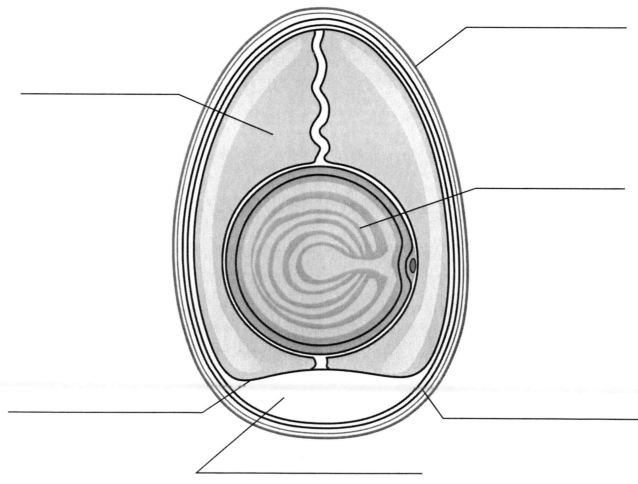

Language Learning–Regular Past Tense Verbs

Directions: Read the list of verbs from the book. Write the past tense of each verb.

Language Hints!

- Verbs are action words. They tell what happens.
- The past tense of verbs show that action happened in the past instead of right now.
- Many verbs add *–d* or *–ed* to form the past tense.

Present Tense	Past Tense
1. gasp	*gasped*
2. poke	
3. boast	
4. repeat	
5. tie	
6. plunge	
7. kill	
8. tremble	
9. agree	
10. sniff	

Name _____ Date _____

Story Elements-Characters

Directions: Choose four animal characters and write their names on the lines. Then, create playing cards for them. List important information about each one and describe his or her relationship with Wilbur.

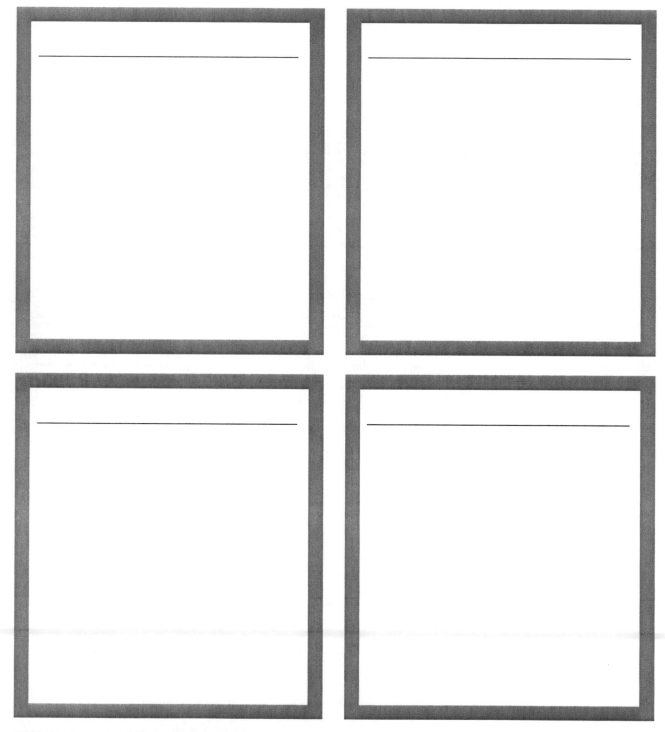

Story Elements–Plot

Directions: Draw a cartoon of Wilbur's attempt to make a web. Include speech bubbles for the characters' thoughts and/or speech. Plan on scrap paper first since you can show just six images.

ılary Overview

Key and phrases from this section are provided below with definitions and sentences about how the words are used in the story. Introduce and discuss these important vocabulary words with students. If you think these words or other words in the story warrant more time devoted to them, there are suggestions in the introduction for other vocabulary activities (page 5).

Word	Definition	Sentence about Text
surly (ch. 10)	cranky; unfriendly	Miserable Templeton speaks in a **surly** tone of voice.
astride (ch. 10)	sitting with one leg on each side	Charlotte rests **astride** her web, thinking of a way to help Wilbur.
bestirred (ch. 10)	moved to action; roused oneself	After quietly thinking for a long time, Charlotte **bestirs** herself.
exertions (ch. 11)	physical or mental efforts	Charlotte's **exertions** in writing on the web leave her exhausted.
sermon (ch. 11)	a talk given by a religious leader, usually during a church service	The minister says he will give a **sermon** about the miracle of the web.
buckboards (ch. 11)	open, four-wheeled wooden vehicles that are pulled by horses	Farmers come in **buckboards** to see the famous spider web.
idiosyncrasy (ch. 12)	a distinctive, individual way of thinking or behaving	The gander's **idiosyncrasy** is to repeat words three times.
access (ch. 12)	a way of getting near to something	Templeton has **access** to the things in the Zuckermans 'dump.
destiny (ch. 12)	the events that will happen to a person in the future	The old sheep points out that Templeton's **destiny** is linked to Wilbur's.
radiant (ch. 13)	glowing; bright and shining	Templeton finds a strip of soap flake packaging that reads, "With New **Radiant** Action."
writhing (ch. 13)	repeatedly twisting one's body from side to side	Wilbur does a **writhing**, twisting backflip to entertain Charlotte.
incessant (ch. 14)	not stopping; without ceasing	Dr. Dorian tells Mrs. Arable that people are **incessant** talkers.

Note: In chapter 12, Charlotte refers negatively to St. Vitus's Dance. This is a disorder now called Sydenham's chorea that affects mostly children.

Vocabulary Activity

Directions: Complete each sentence below using one of the words in the boxes. One word is not used.

surly	exertion	access	sermon
radiant	bestirs	destiny	idiosyncrasy

1. The gander exhibits his _____ when he says, "Here, here, here!"

2. The third message that Charlotte writes in her web is _____.

3. The minister preaches a _____ about the words in the web.

4. Templeton is crabby and speaks in a _____ tone of voice.

5. Charlotte _____ herself and begins work on her special web.

6. It takes a lot of _____ on Charlotte's part to write words in her web.

7. Templeton has _____ to magazines in the Zuckermans' dump.

Directions: Answer the question.

8. When and why does Wilbur **writhe**?

_____

_____

Analyzing the Literature

Provided below are discussion questions you can use in small groups, with the whole class, or for written assignments. Each question is written at two levels so that you can choose the right question for each group of students. For each question, a few key points are provided for your reference as you discuss the book with students.

Story Element	Level 1	Level 2	Key Discussion Points
Character	Is Charlotte a good friend to Wilbur? Yes	What does Charlotte do that proves she is a loyal friend to Wilbur?	Charlotte is a good and loyal friend to Wilbur. First, she promises to save his life when he is overcome with dread. Then, she spends a lot of time thinking of a plan. Finally, she spends time and a great deal of effort writing the words *some pig, terrific,* and *radiant* in her web.
Plot	How does Avery try to capture Charlotte?	How would it affect the story if Avery caught Charlotte?	Avery thinks Charlotte is a fine-looking spider. He decides to capture her by using a stick to knock her into a candy box. Luckily, he does not succeed. If Avery had caught Charlotte, she would not have had the chance to write the words in the web that save Wilbur's life. In addition, Wilbur would've been heartbroken to lose his friend.
Plot	Why does Mrs. Arable visit Dr. Dorian?	Why is Dr. Dorian's reaction to Mrs. Arable's questions important?	Mrs. Arable is afraid that Fern is spending too much time at the Zuckerman barn. She is also disturbed because Fern says she can understand what the animals say. After Dr. Dorian calms Mrs. Arable down and says that Fern is healthy and normal, Mrs. Arable decides to allow Fern to continue visiting Wilbur.
Setting	In chapter 11, where are Charlotte's web located?	How is the position of Charlotte's web in chapter 11 essential to the story?	Charlotte's webs sit right in the doorway of Wilbur's pigpen. They glisten and glow with dew in the morning light. Since the webs are right over the pigpen, Wilbur can stand and sit underneath them. This way, the webs have a bigger impact when people come to see them.

Reader Response

Think

Charlotte and Wilbur quickly become best friends. Think about your own friends. What makes each of them a good friend?

Opinion Writing Prompt

Would you rather be friends with Charlotte or Wilbur? Explain why.

_____

_____

_____

_____

_____

_____

_____

_____

_____

_____

Name _____ Date _____

Guided Close Reading

Closely reread part of Mrs. Arable's conversation with Dr. Dorian in chapter 14. Start with, "Have you heard about the words . . . ." Stop with, "I can give you my word on that."

Directions: Think about these questions. In the space below, write ideas or draw pictures as you think. Be ready to share your answers.

---

❶ Dr. Dorian thinks all spider webs are miraculous. Find evidence to support this statement.

---

❷ What words from the text tell how Mrs. Arable feels about the words in the web?

---

❸ How, according to the text, does Dr. Dorian feel about talking animals?

Making Connections—Domesticated Animals and Wild Animals

Directions: A domesticated animal is one that humans have tamed, such as a pig. A wild animal is one that humans have not tamed, such as a fox. In each column at the bottom of the page, write the living conditions that describe that type of animal. (One choice goes in both of the columns!)

Living Conditions

food provided (D)	(D) human-made surroundings
receive medical care (D)	(W) have to find food
free to go anywhere (W)	(W) can be killed and eaten
kept in a pen (D)	(W) don't receive any medical care

Domesticated Animal

food provided

~~der~~ medical car

Wild Animal

Name _____ Date _____

Language Learning–Past Tense Verbs That Change Form

Directions: The past tense verbs underlined below changed their form. Read each sentence. Then, write the present tense of the underlined verb(s).

Language Hints!

- Many verbs add a *–d* or *–ed* to create the past tense.
- Other verbs **change their form**, as when *sleep* changes to *slept* and *say* changes to *said*.

Past Tense Verb	Present Tense Verb(s)
1. "If I can fool a bug, I can fool a man," Charlotte <u>thought</u>.	*thinks*
2. He <u>took</u> a deep breath and jumped.	take
3. Avery <u>threw</u> the rope swing to his sister.	throw
4. Avery noticed the spider web and <u>saw</u> Charlotte.	sees
5. The children <u>went</u> to the field, picked raspberries, and <u>ate</u> them.	go eat
6. Fern <u>held</u> her nose and <u>ran</u> toward the house.	holding /hold running /run
7. Wilbur <u>stood</u> in his trough, drooling with hunger.	stand standing
8. Mr. Zuckerman <u>spoke</u> to his wife about the words in the web.	speak speaking

Story Elements-Plot

Directions: Fill in the graphic organizer below. Describe the event that will come to be known as "the miracle."

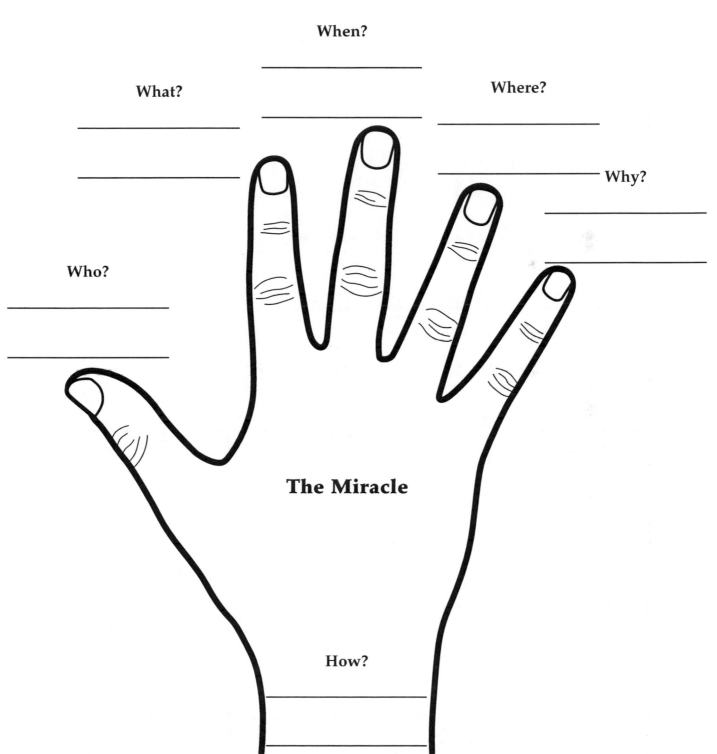

When?

_____

What?

_____

_____

Where?

_____

Why?

_____

_____

Who?

_____

_____

The Miracle

How?

_____

_____

Story Elements–Setting

Directions: Mr. Zuckerman has the best swing in the county. Reread the description of how the local children use the swing. Then cut out the strips below. Put them in the right order, and paste them on a piece of paper.

sail through the barn door going a mile a minute

straddle the knot so it acts as a seat

sail out again (not so far this time)

climb a ladder to the hayloft

jump off and let somebody else try it

drop down out of the sky and come sailing back

take a deep breath and jump

stand at the edge and look down

sail in again, then out, then in, then out

zoom upward and look at the clouds

Vocabulary Overview

Key words and phrases from this section are provided below with definitions and sentences about how the words are used in the story. Introduce and discuss these important vocabulary words with students. If you think these words or other words in the story warrant more time devoted to them, there are suggestions in the introduction for other vocabulary activities (page 5).

Word	Definition	Sentence about Text
monotonous (ch. 15)	spoken in the same tone without any variation	The crickets sing the same **monotonous** song over and over.
distinguish (ch. 15)	to stand out as special in some way	Wilbur hopes to **distinguish** himself at the fair and win some prize money.
forsake (ch. 15)	to leave alone; abandon	Wilbur knows that Charlotte will not **forsake** him when he needs her most.
veritable (ch. 16)	actual; real	The old sheep tells the rat that he will find a **veritable** feast at the fair.
surpass (ch. 16)	to go beyond; to be better than	The sheep predicts that the food at the fair will **surpass** Templeton's wildest dreams.
lacerated (ch. 16)	torn or deeply cut	The rat tells Wilbur to be careful not to step on or **lacerate** him.
swollen (ch. 17)	larger in size; puffed up	Wilbur notices that Charlotte is **swollen** and doesn't seem well.
detected (ch. 18)	noticed; discovered	Templeton's fine nose **detects** many delicious odors in the air.
deviled ham (ch. 18)	a canned spread made from ground-up ham and spices	Templeton eats the remains of a **deviled ham** sandwich.
languishing (ch. 19)	becoming weak	Charlotte tells Wilbur that she is **languishing** and feeling her age.
husky (ch. 19)	hoarse; rough	When he finally drags himself back to the stall, Templeton's voice is rough and **husky**.
carousing (ch. 19)	eating, drinking, and being merry	Templeton is tired and surly after his long night of **carousing**.

Name _____ Date _____

Vocabulary Activity

Directions: Read each word from the story below. Think of what it means. Then, draw a line to match the word to its synonym.

Language Hints!

- A synonym is a word that has the same meaning as another word.

- *Big* is a synonym for *large*. *Moist* is a synonym for *damp*.

Words from the Story	Synonyms
1. monotonous	noticed
2. forsake	hoarse
3. languishing	boring
4. husky	actual
5. detected	exceed
6. surpass	weakening
7. veritable	abandon

Directions: Answer this question.

8. Why is Charlotte **swollen**?

_____

_____

Analyzing the Literature

Provided below are discussion questions you can use in small groups, with the whole class, or for written assignments. Each question is written at two levels so that you can choose the right question for each group of students. For each question, a few key points are provided for your reference as you discuss the book with students.

Story Element	Level 1	Level 2	Key Discussion Points
Character	What does Charlotte say when Wilbur asks her to go to the fair?	Why doesn't Charlotte want to go to the fair? Why does she decide to go anyway?	Charlotte tells Wilbur that she does not think she can go to the fair. She senses that the time is coming for her to create her egg sac, and she wants to be at home in the barn. Wilbur is so distressed by this that Charlotte relents. She wants to help her friend even though she knows it will be difficult for her.
Character	Why does Templeton go to the fair with Wilbur and Charlotte?	What kind of motivation successfully convinces Templeton to go to the fair?	Templeton says he has no interest in the fair and will not go to help Charlotte and Wilbur. However, the old sheep tells Templeton that the fair will be a "rat's paradise," a feast unlike any he's ever experienced. Templeton is a glutton and wants to stuff himself with food. He is motivated by greed, not by friendship.
Plot	Why do the Arables and Zuckermans get upset when they see a blue tag on Uncle's pen at the fair?	How do the families react when they realize Wilbur did not win first prize?	The blue tag indicates that Uncle has won first prize pig. Everyone had hoped—and maybe even expected—that Wilbur would earn that prize. The Zuckermans and Arables are stunned and sorely disappointed. However, they then give Wilbur a buttermilk bath. This shows that they are still proud of him, even though he did not win.
Setting	How does Fern act differently at the fair than she does at home?	Explain how the fair has a major influence on Fern.	Fern is allowed to go off without her parents at the fair. She explores, buys treats, and rides the Ferris wheel with Henry Fussy. Fern becomes interested in Henry—in fact, more interested in him than she is in Wilbur. She stops spending time with the animals. It seems the fair sparks some new maturity and interests in Fern.

Name _____ Date _____

Reader Response

Think

At the fair, Fern enjoys riding the Ferris wheel. Think about a fair or an amusement park you have visited.

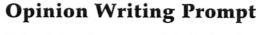

Opinion Writing Prompt

Which ride do you think is the best? Describe the ride in detail. Explain why you think it's the best.

_____

_____

_____

_____

_____

_____

_____

_____

_____

_____

Guided Close Reading

Closely reread the part in chapter 16 where Wilbur is about to be put into the crate. Start with, "Well, said Mrs. Zuckerman . . . ." Stop at, "He rose slowly to his feet, while the geese cheered."

Directions: Think about these questions. In the space below, write ideas or draw pictures as you think. Be ready to share your answers.

❶ According to the text, why does Wilbur faint?

❷ Based on the events in the story, is it a compliment when Templeton says, "What fantastic creatures boys are!"?

❸ How, specifically, does Fern react to Wilbur's struggles?

Name _____ Date _____

Making Connections–Navajo Textiles

Lurvy is delighted when he wins a Navajo blanket at the fair. The Navajo are American Indians who live in the Southwest. For hundreds of years, they have grown sheep and used their wool to weave blankets and rugs. Their work uses line patterns.

Directions: Look at pictures of Navajo blankets in books or online. Notice the colors used. Color the Navajo blanket below using those colors.

Name _____ Date _____

Language Learning–Adjectives

Directions: Circle the words in the Word Bank that are adjectives. Write each one in an oval on the word web below. Then, add a noun from the Word Bank to match each adjective. Plan ahead so every adjective is paired with a logical noun.

Language Hints!

- Adjectives are words that describe nouns.

- Adjectives may tell which one, which kind, what color, or how many.

Word Bank

large	quarters	beautiful	sheep
midway	old	five	pig
hot	pink	day	dusty
ears	web	famous	crate

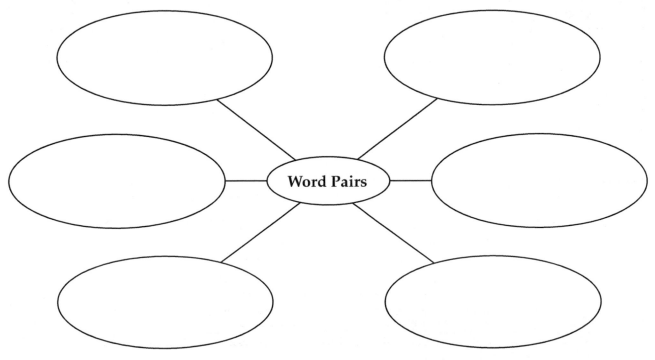

Name _____ Date _____

Story Elements-Setting

Directions: Think about some of the settings in this section of *Charlotte's Web*. Write the settings below. Write at least three details about each of the settings.

Setting	Details
	• • •
	• • •
	• • •
	• • •

Story Elements-Character

Directions: Create an advertisement to get people to come to the fair to see Wilbur, Zuckerman's Famous Pig.

Vocabulary Overview

Key words and phrases from this section are provided below with definitions and sentences about how the words are used in the story. Introduce and discuss these important vocabulary words with students. If you think these words or other words in the story warrant more time devoted to them, there are suggestions in the introduction for other vocabulary activities (page 5).

Word	Definition	Sentence about Text
pompous (ch. 20)	the attitude of one who believes he is better, smarter, and more important than others	The man uses a **pompous** voice to make the special announcement at the fair.
phenomenon (ch. 20)	something that exists but may be hard to fully explain	People agree that the words in the web are an amazing **phenomenon.**
supernatural (ch. 20)	unable to be explained by science or the laws of nature	The announcer says that the words in the web must be the result of **supernatural** forces.
trifle (ch. 21)	to a small degree; a little bit	Charlotte says that she improved her own life a **trifle** by helping Wilbur.
sentiments (ch. 21)	feelings or emotions	Wilbur expresses his **sentiments** to Charlotte before she dies.
desolation (ch. 21)	grief and extreme misery	When Charlotte says she is about to die, Wilbur throws himself to the floor in **desolation.**
accompany (ch. 21)	to go somewhere with another; to be a companion	Charlotte is too weak to **accompany** Wilbur back home.
solemn (ch. 21)	sincere; serious	Wilbur makes a **solemn** vow that he will forever let the rat eat first from the slops.
updraft (ch. 22)	an upward current or flow of air	The tiny baby spiders fly away on the warm **updraft.**
hallowed (ch. 22)	highly respected; blessed	Wilbur calls Charlotte's old spot a **hallowed** doorway.
tranquil (ch. 22)	peaceful and quiet	Wilbur lives the rest of his happy, **tranquil** life in the barn.
garrulous (ch. 22)	overly talkative	Wilbur appreciates his barn friends, even the **garrulous** geese.

Vocabulary Activity

Directions: Read each word from the story below. Think of what it means. Then, draw a line to match the word to its antonym. An antonym is a word that has the opposite meaning of another word. *Wet* is an antonym for *dry*. *Big* is an antonym for *small*.

Words from the Story	Antonym
1. pompous	silly
2. desolation	noisy
3. trifle	ordinary
4. solemn	quiet
5. tranquil	joy
6. garrulous	humble
7. supernatural	a lot

Directions: Answer this question.

8. Why doesn't Charlotte **accompany** Wilbur back to the barn?

_____

_____

Analyzing the Literature

Provided below are discussion questions you can use in small groups, with the whole class, or for written assignments. Each question is written at two levels so that you can choose the right question for each group of students. For each question, a few key points are provided for your reference as you discuss the book with students.

Story Element	Level 1	Level 2	Key Discussion Points
Character	How does Avery act in front of the crowds during Wilbur's ceremony?	What does Avery's behavior during the prize ceremony tell us about him?	After Avery gets wet, he acts like a clown in front of the whole crowd. The louder the applause, the more Avery shows off. He dumps water on himself and makes faces. Avery obviously loves being in the spotlight and wants to be the center of attention.
Character	How does Wilbur cope with losing Charlotte?	What keeps Wilbur from being overwhelmed by grief when Charlotte dies?	After losing Charlotte, Wilbur focuses on the future. He watches over her egg sac with great care. He is able to cope without his friend because he believes that in the spring he will have 514 new friends, all of them Charlotte's children. "Life is always a rich and steady time when you are waiting for something . . ."
Plot	Why is it good that three of Charlotte's daughters stay with Wilbur?	What development at the end of the story helps it end on a happy note?	Wilbur would be depressed and lonely if all of Charlotte's children left him. When he awakes after crying himself to sleep, he is delighted to find that Joy, Aranea, and Nellie have decided to spin their webs in his doorway. This lets the story end on a happy note. The reader knows that Wilbur will never be lonely again.
Setting	Why does Charlotte stay behind at the fairgrounds?	The saddest event in the book occurs at the fairgrounds. Explain.	Charlotte is near death, and she does not have the strength to get herself to the crate. She does not even have enough silk left to lower herself to the ground. Wilbur is devastated, but he has no choice but to leave his friend behind. Therefore, loving, loyal Charlotte is all alone in the pigpen at the fair when she dies.

Reader Response

Think

Wilbur is extremely sad when he realizes that Charlotte's children are flying away on the updraft. Think about a time when you felt very sad.

Informative/Explanatory Writing Prompt

Write three ideas for things you can do to help someone who is feeling very sad feel better. Explain each idea thoroughly.

_____

_____

_____

_____

_____

_____

_____

_____

_____

Name _____ Date _____

Guided Close Reading

Closely reread the section of chapter 21 where Charlotte and Wilbur have an emotional conversation. Start at the beginning of the chapter. Stop with, "And I thank you for your generous sentiments."

Directions: Think about these questions. In the space below, write ideas or draw pictures as you think. Be ready to share your answers.

❶ Based on the text, why does Charlotte feel peaceful?

❷ Wilbur asks Charlotte why she has done so much to help him. What answer does she give him?

❸ In the text, what does Wilbur say he would do for Charlotte if he could?

Making Connections—
The Life Cycle of a Barn Spider

All spiders start as eggs, hatch as spiderlings, and molt before becoming adults. When a spider molts, its exoskeleton cracks open. The spider has grown too large for it. The spider climbs out and crawls away. After mating, the male spider dies. After laying her eggs, the female spider dies. Most barn spiders live for a year, so Charlotte is already an adult when she meets Wilbur.

Directions: Label each stage of the barn spider life cycle in the diagram below. Use the Internet or library to help you.

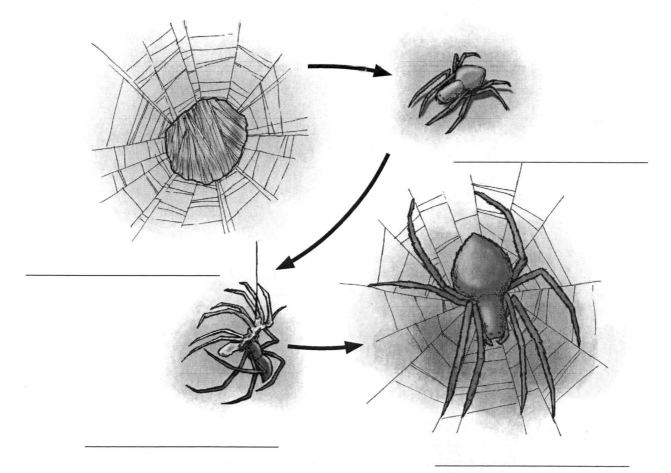

Language Learning-Adverbs

Directions: Use the adverb that best fits in each sentence from the story. Read all the choices and sentences first. Each word is used once. You can use the book to help if you need to.

Language Hints!

- Adverbs are words that describe verbs (action words) or adjectives (words that describe nouns).

- Adverbs often end in –ly.

immediately	busily	rudely	truly
patiently	deeply	gladly	suddenly

1. "The truck carrying this _____ extraordinary pig is approaching the grandstand."

2. "Avery knelt in the dirt beside the pig, _____ stroking him and showing off."

3. "When Wilbur heard the crowd cheering and clapping, he _____ fainted."

4. "Finding himself wet, Avery _____ started to act like a clown."

5. "Mr. Zuckerman felt that it was _____ satisfying to win a prize in front of a lot of people."

6. "Wilbur said, 'Charlotte, I would _____ give my life for you.'"

7. "Templeton snapped, 'Can't a rat catch a wink of sleep without being _____ popped into the air?'"

8. "Wilbur _____ waited for the end of winter and the coming of the little spiders."

Story Elements–Character

Directions: Wilbur is lucky to have two wonderful friends early in his life. His first friend is Fern. Later, he meets Charlotte. Think about Wilbur and his two friends. Fill in the chart below. On the left, list ways that Fern's friendship improves Wilbur's life. On the right, list ways that Charlotte touches his life.

Fern	Charlotte

Name _____ Date _____

Story Elements–Plot

Directions: Fill in the graphic organizer below based on the events from chapters 20–22.

Cause	Effect
Wilbur promises to let Templeton eat first forever. ➡	
➡	The spiderlings hatch in Wilbur's pen.
The spiderlings become aeronauts. ➡	
➡	Wilbur is happy.

Post-Reading Theme Thoughts

Directions: Choose a main character from *Charlotte's Web*. Pretend you are that character. Draw a picture of a happy face or a sad face to show how the character would feel about each statement below. Then, use words to explain your picture.

Character I Chose: _____

Statement	How Do You Feel? ☺ ☹	Explain Your Answer
Spending time with animals can be enjoyable.		
A loyal friend can be hard to find.		
Sometimes we have to say good-bye to a friend.		
There is great joy simply in being alive.		

Culminating Activity: Writing Scripts

Directions: Reproduce the stick puppet patterns from pages 61–64 on cardstock or construction paper. Have students use markers to color the patterns and cut them out. Then, glue each pattern to a tongue depressor or craft stick.

Ways to Use the Stick Puppets

- Let students write their own scripts that retell events in *Charlotte's Web* in their own words. Doing so will help them understand how books get turned into plays and movie scripts.

- Have students create a new adventure for Wilbur using the stick puppets.

- Have students write an epilogue or sequel for the book.

- Have students work in pairs or small groups to create a script and stage it for the rest of the class or a class of younger students.

- Have students decorate a large cardboard box for a stage. Record the performances and have them playing on a computer screen during an open house or parent conferences. You can also upload the performances online and send home a link to parents.

Culminating Activity: Writing Scripts *(cont.)*

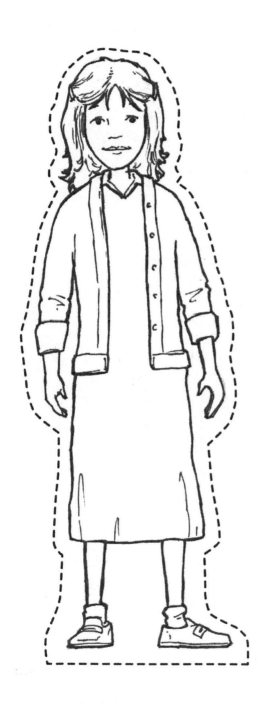

Note: The spider can be Charlotte, Joy, Aranea, or Nellie.

Culminating Activity: Writing Scripts (cont.)

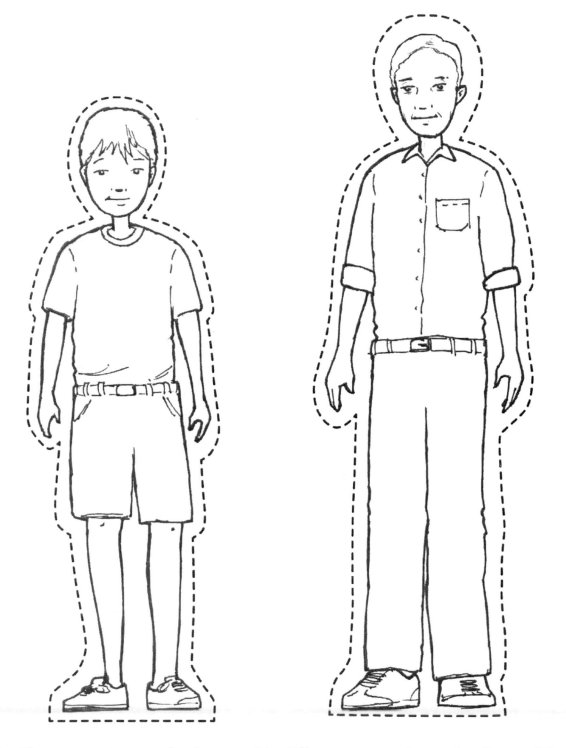

Note: The man pattern can be decorated in different ways to be used as Lurvy, Mr. Zuckerman, Mr. Arable, Dr. Dorian, or the judge who gives Wilbur the award.

Culminating Activity: Writing Scripts *(cont.)*

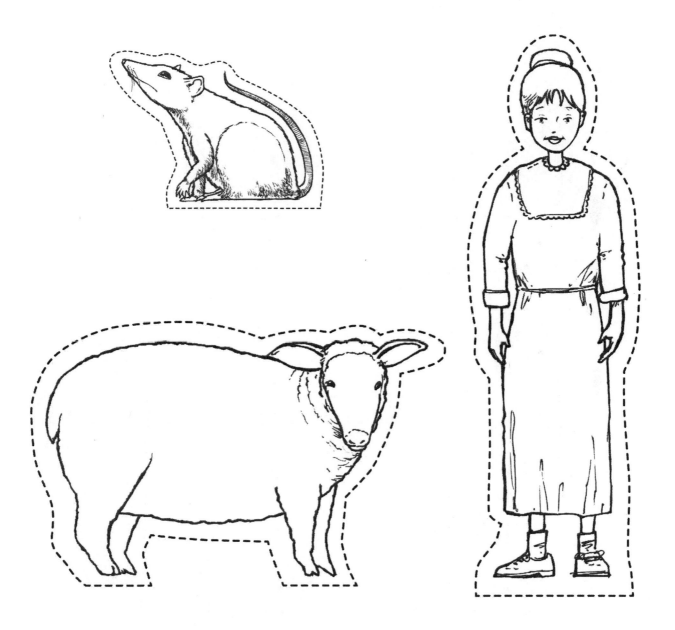

Note: The woman pattern can be decorated in different ways to be used as Mrs. Arable or Mrs. Zuckerman.

Culminating Activity: Writing Scripts *(cont.)*

Comprehension Assessment

Directions: Fill in the bubble for the best response to each question.

Section 1

1. What does Wilbur do while he lives under the apple tree at the Arables' home?

   (A) He drinks milk from a trough.

   (B) He sleeps under the straw in his box.

   (C) He escapes through a gap in the fence.

   (D) He runs away and ends up in the cold brook.

Section 2

2. What does Templeton do that shows he isn't always surly?

   (E) He puts the rotten goose egg in his lair under Wilbur's trough.

   (F) He always waits until Wilbur is done before eating from the trough.

   (G) He would kill a gosling if he could get away with it.

   (H) He gets a string and ties it around Wilbur's tail.

Section 3

3. What does Avery say right after he falls into Wilbur's trough?

   (A) "What a stink! Let's get out of here!"

   (B) "That's a fine spider and I'm going to capture it."

   (C) "I want to live in a tree with my frog."

   (D) "Let's swing in the swing!"

Comprehension Assessment (cont.)

Section 4

4. Why does Mrs. Arable go to visit Dr. Dorian?

_____

_____

_____

_____

_____

Section 5

5. What does Charlotte say that lets Wilbur know he can safely carry her egg sac in his mouth?

Ⓐ "It is my egg sac, my *mangum opus.*"

Ⓑ "This egg sac is my great work—the finest thing I have ever made."

Ⓒ "It's waterproof so the eggs inside will be warm and dry."

Ⓓ "Yes, it *is* pretty."

Response to Literature: Sensory Details from
Charlotte's Web

Directions: E. B. White's wonderfully descriptive writing helps you to "make a movie in your mind." You can almost see, smell, and hear the events in *Charlotte's Web*. Draw a detailed picture of your favorite scene from the story. Make your picture neat and colorful. Then, answer the questions on the next page about your scene.

Response to Literature: Sensory Details from
Charlotte's Web (cont.)

1. What can you see, smell, and hear in this scene?

   _____

   _____

   _____

   _____

2. Why do you think this scene is special?

   _____

   _____

   _____

   _____

3. What happens next in the story?

   _____

   _____

   _____

   _____

Response to Literature Rubric

Directions: Use this rubric to evaluate student responses.

Great Job	Good Work	Keep Trying
☐ You answered all three questions completely. You included many details.	☐ You answered all three questions.	☐ You did not answer all three questions.
☐ Your handwriting is very neat. There are no spelling errors.	☐ Your handwriting can be neater. There are some spelling errors.	☐ Your handwriting is not very neat. There are many spelling errors.
☐ Your picture is neat and fully colored.	☐ Your picture is neat and some of it is colored.	☐ Your picture is not very neat and/or fully colored.
☐ Creativity is clear in both the picture and the writing.	☐ Creativity is clear in either the picture or the writing.	☐ There is not much creativity in either the picture or the writing.

Teacher Comments: _____

_____

_____

_____

Answer Key

The responses provided here are just examples of what students may answer. Many accurate responses are possible for the questions throughout this unit.

Vocabulary Activity—Section 1:
Chapters 1–4 (page 15)

1. Avery thinks that Wilbur is a miserable **specimen** of a pig because he is as small as a white rat.

Guided Close Reading—Section 1:
Chapters 1–4 (page 18)

1. "Every animal stirred and lifted its head and became excited to know that one of his friends had got free and was no longer penned up or tied fast."
2. "Wilbur didn't know what to do or which way to run. It seemed as though everybody was after him. 'If this is what it's like to be free,' he thought, 'I believe I'd rather be penned up in my own yard.'"
3. Mrs. Zuckerman yells that the pig's out. The men come running and so does Mrs. Zuckerman. They all try to encircle Wilbur.

Making Connections—Section 1:
Chapters 1–4 (page 19)

Answers will vary, but should include foods mentioned in the text. The barn cat is a carnivore who eats mice, fish, and birds. For Templeton, both a meat and a plant must be listed. The sheep is a herbivore who eats hay, grass, and corn.

Language Learning—Section 1:
Chapters 1–4 (page 20)

- In noun trough: farmer, sheep, barn, pigpen, rat, goose
- In proper noun trough: Lurvy, Wilbur, Templeton, Avery, Mrs. Arable, Mr. Zuckerman

Story Elements—Section 1:
Chapters 1–4 (page 21)

Somebody wants	But	So
Mr. Arable wants to kill the runt pig.	Fern begs him not to and says it is unjust.	Mr. Arable gives the pig to Fern to raise.
Fern wants to keep the baby pig.	Mr. Arable sells Wilbur to Mr. Zuckerman.	Wilbur goes to live in the Zuckerman barn.
Wilbur is lonely and wants a friend.	The lamb refuses to play with him.	A voice promises to be Wilbur's friend.

Vocabulary Activity—Section 2:
Chapters 5–9 (page 24)

- The spider injects an **anaesthetic** into each bug that **blunders** into her web.
- When the sheep says that Wilbur will die, the pig responds with **hysterics**.
- Templeton seems happy to **oblige** when Wilbur asks him for a piece of string.
- The mowing machine leaves **swathes** of hay in the field.
- Charlotte's **inheritance** is the ability to build a web and trap flies.

1. Templeton lacks **scruples**, and the book states that all the animals are aware of it.

Guided Close Reading—Section 2:
Chapters 5–9 (page 27)

1. Charlotte is a trapper because her mother and her mother's mother and all her family have been trappers for thousands of years.
2. "'It's a miserable inheritance, ' said Wilbur gloomily." He is sad because his new friend is so bloodthirsty. "'It's cruel,' replied Wilbur."
3. "Do you realize that if I didn't catch bugs and eat them, bugs would increase and multiply and get so numerous that they'd destroy the earth, wipe out everything?"

Making Connections—Section 2:
Chapters 5–9 (page 28)

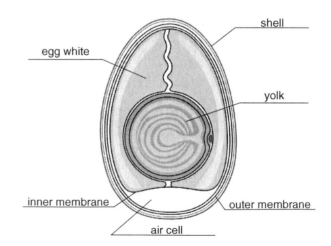

Language Learning—Section 2:
Chapters 5–9 (page 29)

1. gasped
2. poked
3. boasted
4. repeated
5. tied
6. plunged
7. killed
8. trembled
9. agreed
10. sniffed

Vocabulary Activity—Section 3:
Chapters 10–14 (page 33)

1. idiosyncrasy
2. radiant
3. sermon
4. surly
5. bestirs
6. exertion
7. access
8. Wilbur **writhes** when Charlotte asks him to do a back flip in order to prove he is radiant.

Guided Close Reading—Section 3:
Chapters 10–14 (page 36)

1. "Nobody pointed out that the web itself is a miracle. . . . Who taught a spider? A young spider knows how to spin a web without any instructions from anybody. Don't you regard that as a miracle?"
2. "I don't understand how those words got into the web. I don't understand, and I don't like what I can't understand."
3. "I never heard one say anything, but that proves nothing. It is quite possible that an animal has spoken civilly to me and that I didn't catch the remark because I wasn't paying attention . . . If Fern says that the animals in Zuckerman's barn talk, I'm quite ready to believe her."

Making Connections—Section 3:
Chapters 10–14 (page 37)

Domesticated Animal	Wild Animal
food provided	have to find food
kept in a pen	free to go anywhere
receive medical care	don't receive any medical care
can be killed and eaten	can be killed and eaten
human-made surroundings	

Language Learning—Section 3:
Chapters 10–14 (page 38)

1. thinks
2. takes
3. throws
4. sees
5. go; eat
6. holds; runs
7. stands
8. speaks

Story Elements—Section 3:
Chapters 10–14 (page 39)

- Who?—Charlotte
- What?—Writes SOME PIG in her web
- When?—overnight
- Where?—above Wilbur's doorway
- Why?—to save Wilbur's life
- How?—with her spinnerets and silk

Story Elements—Section 3:
Chapters 10–14 (page 40)

- climb a ladder to the hayloft
- stand at the edge and look down
- straddle the knot so it acts as a seat
- take a deep breath and jump
- sail through the barn door going a mile a minute
- zoom upward and look at the clouds
- drop down out of the sky and come sailing back
- sail out again (not so far this time)
- sail in again, then out, then in, then out
- jump off and let somebody else try it

Vocabulary Activity—Section 4:
Chapters 15–19 (page 42)

1. monotonous, boring
2. forsake, abandon
3. languishing, weakening
4. husky, hoarse
5. detected, noticed
6. surpass, exceed
7. veritable, actual
8. Charlotte is **swollen** because her body is filled with eggs.

Guided Close Reading—Section 4:
Chapters 15–19 (page 45)

1. Wilbur faints after he hears Mr. Arable say, "You'll get some extra good ham and bacon, Homer, when it comes time to kill that pig."
2. No, it's not a compliment. Templeton says this when he is worried that Avery will injure him by being silly and crawling around in Wilbur's crate.
3. Fern screams, "He's fading away!" She also hollers at Avery to keep quiet. Her eyes brim with tears.

Making Connections—Section 4:
Chapters 15–19 (page 46)

Having students look at multiple representations will result in their drawing a conclusion about the colors, which are always bold shades of red, orange, white, and black or brown. This is due to the pigments available to the Navajo in the Southwest. One wouldn't see pink, purple, green, blue, or *any* pastel color in Navajo blankets/rugs.

Language Learning—Section 4:
Chapters 15–19 (page 47)

- large crate
- five quarters
- beautiful web
- old sheep
- hot day
- dusty
- pink ears
- famous pig

There are many other combinations that would work, too, as in *famous man, large pig, five ears,* and *dusty quarters.*

Vocabulary Activity—Section 5:
Chapters 20–22 (page 51)

1. pompous, humble
2. desolation, joy
3. trifle, a lot
4. solemn, silly
5. tranquil, noisy
6. garrulous, quiet
7. supernatural, ordinary
8. Charlotte doesn't **accompany** Wilbur because she is too weak to climb down and get into the crate.

Guided Close Reading—Section 5:
Chapters 20–22 (page 54)

1. Charlotte feels peaceful because she knows she has succeeded in saving Wilbur. "Your future is assured. You will live secure and safe, Wilbur. Nothing can harm you now."
2. "'You have been my friend,' replied Charlotte. 'That in itself is a tremendous thing. I wove my webs for you because I liked you.'"
3. Wilbur says, "I would gladly give my life for you—I really would."

Making Connections—Section 5:
Chapters 20–22 (page 55)

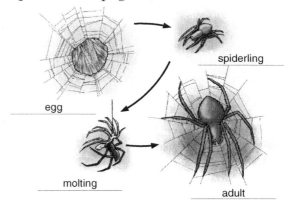

Language Learning—Section 5:
Chapters 20–22 (page 56)

1. truly
2. busily
3. suddenly
4. immediately
5. deeply
6. gladly
7. rudely
8. patiently

Story Elements—Section 5:
Chapters 20–22 (page 58)

Cause	Effect
Wilbur promises to let Templeton eat first forever.	**Templeton gets Charlotte's egg sac and puts it into Wilbur's crate.**
Wilbur puts the egg sac in a protected spot in his pigpen.	The spiderlings hatch in Wilbur's pen.
The spiderlings become aeronauts.	**Wilbur is distraught and cries himself to sleep.**
Three spiderlings stay behind to live with Wilbur.	Wilbur is happy.

Comprehension Assessment
(pages 65–66)

1. B He sleeps under the straw in his box.
2. H He gets a string and ties it around Wilbur's tail.
3. A "What a stink! Let's get out of here!"
4. Mrs. Arable visits Dr. Dorian because she is worried about Fern and wants his advice. Fern has told her that the animals talk, and she understands what they are saying. Mrs. Arable fears that there might be something wrong with Fern and doesn't want her to spend so much time in the Zuckerman barn.
5. C "It's waterproof so the eggs inside will be warm and dry."